Everyday Material

Metal

Andrew Langley

Crabtree Publishing Company

www.crabtreebooks.com

Crabtree Publishing Company

www.crabtreebooks.com

All rights reserved.

Author: Andrew Langley

Editors: Annabel Savery, Adrianna Morganelli

Proofreaders: Michael Hodge, Crystal Sikkens

Project editor: Robert Walker

Designer: Ian Winton

Illustrator: Ian Winton

Picture researcher: Rachel Tisdale

Production coordinator: Margaret Amy Salter

Prepress technician: Margaret Amy Salter

© 2009 Crabtree Publishing Company

Acknowledgements: Corbis: cover main (David Churchill/Arcaid). Discovery Picture Library: 19 inset. Getty Images: 10 (Joel Sartore), 13 (Chris Kapolka), 16 (Dorling Kindersley). Istockphoto: head panels, title page and 21 (Maurice van der Velden), 4 (James Warren), 5 top, 5 bottom and 20 (Sebastian Meckelmann), 6, 11 (Patricia Nelson), 7 (Rob Broek), 9 (Duff Bassett), 12, 14 (Rosen Dukov), 15 (Lars Ziemann), 17, 18 (Oleg Fedorenko), 19 right (Jon Le-Bon). Newscast: 8 (Corus).

Library and Archives Canada Cataloguing in Publication

Langley, Andrew
    Metal / Andrew Langley.

(Everyday materials)
Includes index.
ISBN 978-0-7787-4127-5 (bound).--ISBN 978-0-7787-4134-3 (pbk.)

    1. Metals--Juvenile literature. 2. Metal products--Juvenile literature.
I. Title. II. Series: Langley, Andrew. Everyday materials.

TA459.L35 2008   j620.1'6   C2008-903569-0

Library of Congress Cataloging-in-Publication Data

Langley, Andrew.
    Metal / Andrew Langley.
        p. cm. -- (Everyday materials)
    Includes index.
    ISBN-13: 978-0-7787-4134-3 (pbk. : alk. paper)
    ISBN-10: 0-7787-4134-6 (pbk. : alk. paper)
    ISBN-13: 978-0-7787-4127-5 (reinforced lib. binding : alk. paper)
    ISBN-10: 0-7787-4127-3 (reinforced lib. binding : alk. paper)
    1. Metals--Juvenile literature. I. Title. II. Series.

TA459.L36 2009
620.1'6--dc22
                                          2008024036

Crabtree Publishing Company

www.crabtreebooks.com   1-800-387-7650

Published in Canada
Crabtree Publishing
616 Welland Ave.
St. Catharines, Ontario
L2M 5V6

Published in the United States
Crabtree Publishing
PMB16A
350 Fifth Ave., Suite 3308
New York, NY 10118

First published in 2008
by Wayland
338 Euston Road
London NW1 3BH

Wayland Australia
Level 17/207 Kent Street
Sydney, NSW 2000

Copyright © Wayland 2008

Contents

What is metal?

Metal is a **natural material**. We use metal to make thousands of different things.

San Francisco's Golden Gate Bridge is made of metal.

4

Most kinds of metal are strong and shiny. We can bend and hammer metal into different shapes.

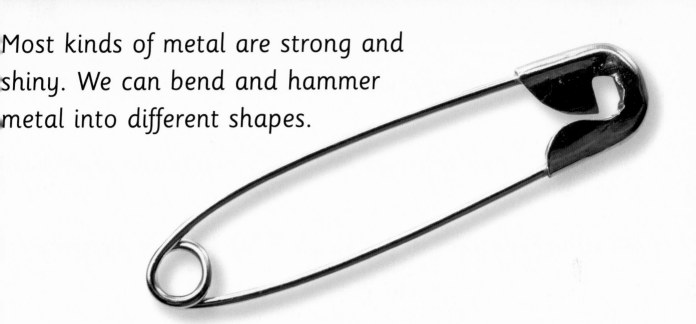

Iron is one of the most common metals in the world. Other metals, such as gold, are rare. We call them **precious** metals.

Eye spy

Look around your classroom. How many metal objects can you see?

Gold rings

Where does metal come from?

Nearly all metal comes out of the ground.
It is mixed with rock and other materials.
We call this mixture
a metal **ore**.

Iron ore

Did you know?

Some metal comes from outer space.
Meteorites falling from the sky
sometimes contain solid iron.

Miners dig metal ore out of the ground. Then they break the ore into pieces.

Making metal

The ore is heated in a tall tower called a **blast furnace**. The metal in the ore melts and becomes a liquid.

8

The other materials in the ore rise to the top of the **molten** metal and form a **scum**. This scum is called **slag**.

Eye spy

When you pour out a fizzy drink, the froth goes to the top. This is because it is lighter than the drink. Slag rises in the same way.

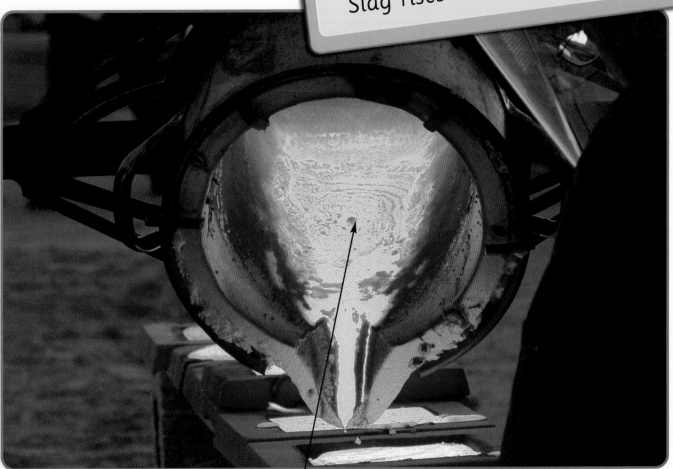

The scum stays on top of the molten metal.

9

Shaping metal

Molten metal is poured into **molds**. As the metal cools, it becomes hard again. It takes on the shape of the mold.

Hot metal can be
hammered or rolled into
many different shapes.
It can also be pulled
through a tiny hole
to make thin wire.

Eye spy

Can you see any
paper clips or staples?
Both of these are
made of wire.

Building with metal

Metal is a strong material. We use it to build very big objects. Many buildings have metal frames. Metal bridges carry roads across wide rivers.

Eye spy

What's the tallest piece of metal near your home? Is it a lamppost? A crane?

12

Even thin metal sheets can be very strong.
Ships, aircraft, and trains are built from
metal. Trains also run on strong metal rails.

Mixing alloys

Iron nails

Iron goes **rusty** if it is left in the air or in water. If we mix iron with some other metals or other materials, it will not rust. This mixture is called an **alloy**.

Eye spy

Fill a small bowl with water. Drop in a teaspoon, a copper coin and a piece of wire wool. The next morning, see which object has gone rusty.

There are many kinds of alloys. Steel is a mixture of iron and **carbon**. It is much stronger than iron on its own.

These oil tanks are made of steel.

Special uses

A **magnet** is made of metal.
It pulls other small metal
objects toward it.

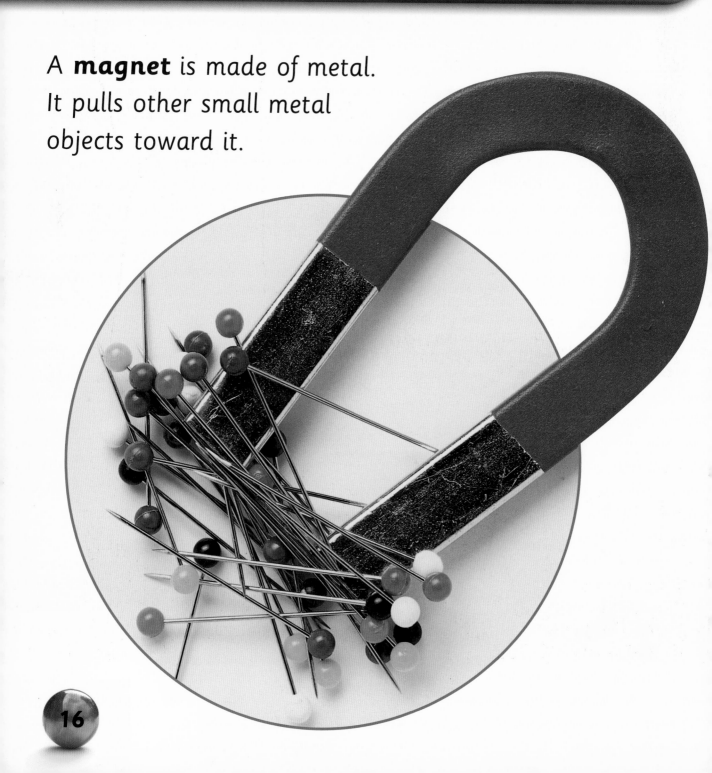

Many machines and
tools are made of
metal. They can
dig tunnels or
cut down trees.

Did you know?

Metal machines
even printed this book.

Recycling metal

Making metal uses
a lot of material and
energy. Metal mines can
spoil huge areas of land.
Some metal factories
pollute the air with
smoke and waste gases.

We can use old metal again. Old cars, cans, and other objects are collected. Then they are cleaned and melted down again.

Squashed metal blocks

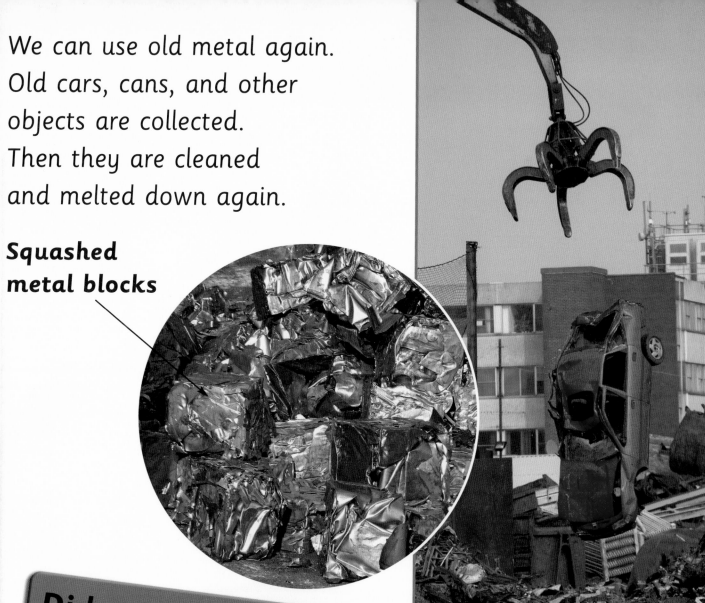

Did you know?

A new car is made partly out of old cars. Nearly half of the metal in it has been used before.

19

Quiz

Questions

1. Which is a precious metal – iron or gold?
2. What is metal ore?
3. What happens in a blast furnace?
4. How is an alloy made?
5. Is a new car made of new metal?

Answers

1. Gold. 2. A mixture of metal, rock, and other materials dug out of the ground. 3. Metal ore is heated. 4. By mixing a metal with other metals or other materials. 5. No – nearly half of it is made of recycled metal.

Metal topic web

Music
Lots of musical instruments are made of metal. Trumpets, tubas, and trombones are all made of a metal called brass.

Geography
Different types of metal can be found all around the world. The countries that produce the most iron are China and Australia.

History
Some ages are named after the metal that people used mostly at that time. There are the Bronze Age and the Iron Age.

Science
Metal is sometimes used by surgeons. They can use it to help join broken bones back together.

English
Read "The Iron Man" by Ted Hughes. It is an exciting story about a man made of metal. He even eats metal!

Glossary

alloy A mixture of a metal with other metals

blast furnace A big oven for melting metal ore. Very hot air is blasted into the furnace

carbon A simple material that is found in all plants and animals

iron One of the most common and useful of all metals

magnet A piece of metal that attracts iron and other metals

meteorite A lump of metal or other materials that reaches Earth from outer space

mold A container that is shaped in a special way. A liquid that is poured in will take the same shape

molten When a material has been heated to a high temperature and becomes a thick liquid

natural material A material found in nature. It is not made by people

ore A rock containing metals mixed with other materials

pollute To damage the environment with harmful substances

precious Very valuable

rusty When a red surface has formed on iron or steel that has been left in the air or in water

scum Waste material that rises to the top of a liquid

slag A mixture of waste materials produced during the making of iron

Further information

Books to read

Amazing Science: Materials. Sally Hewitt. Wayland, 2006.

Find Out About: Find Out About Metal. Henry Pluckrose. Franklin Watts Ltd., 2002.

Raintree Perspectives: Using Materials: How We Use Metal. Chris Oxlade. Raintree Publishers, 2004.

Start-Up Science: Materials. Claire Llewellyn. Evans Brothers Ltd., 2004.

Web sites to visit

BBC Schools
http://www.bbc.co.uk/schools/scienceclips/ages/5_6/sorting_using_mate.shtml
Learn all about different types of materials and their properties.

Think cans
http://www.thinkcans.com/edu_games.htm
Here you can learn all about recycling metal cans.

Recycling guide
http://www.recycling-guide.org.uk/metal.html
http://www.recycling-guide.org.uk/science-aluminium.html
Learn all about how the metal aluminium is recycled.

Index

Printed in China